The Grey Mare Being The Better Steed

The Grey Mare
Being
The Better Steed

Pete Morgan

Secker & Warburg · London

First published in England 1973 by
Martin Secker & Warburg Limited
14 Carlisle Street, London W1N 6NN

Designed by Philip Mann

436 28805 2   (hardcover)
436 28806 0   (paperback)

821
MOR

Printed in Great Britain by Cox & Wyman Limited

For
Spain –
and to her memory

Acknowledgments

Some of these poems have previously appeared in the following publications:—
Akros, Ambit, Capella (Dublin), *Lines Review, New Statesman, Poetry* (Chicago),
Poetry Review, Second Aeon, The Scotsman, Scottish International, Solstice
(Cambridge) and *Spirit* (New Jersey);

In the following collections and anthologies:—
Love Love Love (Corgi Books)
New Poems 1970/71 (P.E.N./Hutchinson)
Poetry: Introduction 2 (Faber & Faber) and
Scottish Poetry 4, 5 & 6 (Edinburgh University Press).

Some of the poems have been broadcast by BBC Radio and Television and have
appeared in two limited edition pamphlets from the Kevin Press (Edinburgh).

Contents

Part I

A theory wound
around the world
is why both men and roots
lap walls

Disguise

Having penetrated my disguise
with lengths of predictable steel
and not a little wit
they
in their indefinite wisdom
scoured my skin with intricate designs
of their own choosing.
Having failed to obliterate
their scars with numberless
additional disguises
and frequent unsuccessful experiments
with Water Fire and Love
I discovered
somewhat later
and quite by accident
that each scar was moveable.
Ahah! Carefully now
and in complete privacy
I moved the markings
over my body and slid them
one by one
into the darkness inside my head
and very much out of sight.

Children
you need no longer be afraid
you can have a laugh with Lumpy now
come closer —
look at my disguise
never let me catch you
looking in my eyes.

The Red Monkey Poems

I
Again the red monkey is in turmoil
beginning to move again
move slowly monkey
Ahah! monkey
Good monkey
monkey
monkey

rien ne va plus, monkey.

II
Again the monkey moves
his hot mouth pressed
against the dome his
pink paws scratch
for a firm
hold

take it easy monkey
take care now monkey
take your time monkey
easy monkey
easy

monkey, don't fall.

III
Inside his hidy-hole
        the red monkey moves
        (like an old time movie)
monkey
monkey
don't dance, monkey

the red monkey is a fair dancer.

IV

Give the red monkey lights
Give the red monkey lights
Give the red monkey lights

he breaks, starry.

V

The small lips suckle at the warm wall
which has no corners

move round the wall/monkey
move round the wall

it is
dark

somewhere.

The Eye

On the seventh day the eye began to re-open
the seeping blood began to clot
the purple bruising turned to blue
but the eye had no sight.

By the tenth day the eye had completely opened
the stitches were finally removed
but there was no pupil and no iris
and still the eye could not see.

On the fourteenth day the sight returned
and only the ugly scar remained.
Daily I schemed avengement for my wound
and planned destruction for my foe.

But each time I put the plan to action
I found the eye closing again
I felt the blood seeping
and the eye had no sight.

The Toft Hill Poem

I am the bull with the rumpus horn
My blood is bitter brine.

Only to the sky
I sing
'I am thine'

I cut my colour till it runs
Yet find no root in blade and bone.

Within my head lie dark and doubt
Yet neither of these gifts I own.

I am the bull with the rumpus horn
My blood is bitter brine —
'To whom can I ring true?'

There is no history to tell
I sail from shade to shade
My only company this song —
This little truth I made:

'My hide was black as ebony
 My eyes they were of jade
Across my horn in false design
 Were gall and wormwood laid.'

Loss of Two Anchors
(Part, The Foist)

> *I'm not going near the water*
> *Am I being good?*
> *My body ain't flat iron*
> *And my soul ain't wood!*

Everything swimming is born to destroy
(pardon the ahem
loud hail the ahoy).

This water's abortive —
percentage of dross
salud to that finding
(more latterly, loss)
salud to the making
salud to the made
salud to the body
and also the blade.

A promise:
for delving
the best gift is lead —
a down on the notion
(apropos the misled)
that up's a correction
that down's a disease
that choice of direction's
compounded of these.

A statement: this walking on
water's a waste
I'm missing some wetness
can't savour the taste —
I need to get higher to spot submarines
and not knowing the latit or longit demeans
the lad who believes not in God
but in dreams
whose passes and suchlike
are stopped by machines.

Back to the water:
Away from the land
(For mazes: the footloose
for guidance: a hand)
so hand is no obstacle
gui:dance is good
(a 'can't' is erratum
for 'shan't' we read
'should').

Everything brightened and shiny ain't new
(the seed no solution
the body a clue
the mirror an impulse
the sowing taboo)
there's nothing as ancient as blue.
There's nothing as old or as bold
as the crow.
Who'll play Survivor?
Who First-To-Go?
My guess is the last one to know.

There's something going on in the depths
I can tell
(all I need is oxygen
perhaps a diving bell)
I couldn't call it easy
to plumb this deep —
got this far with mirrors
and losing sleep.
I tried to get deeper
but the tide came in
and covered up the treasure
and the taste of sin.
And One Hand's Trouble
if it's digging past wet
you're after.

So maze is no ocean
so wave is no stone
(and man as a man
is also a bone).

We're anything bending —
(and looks are nothing
when you've got this far
be it cut or be it scar) —
We're anything bending under the sun
estuary, tributary, peninsula —
but not Fun.
Fun's the last thing we're at
and what we want to know is ...
what we want to know is ...
the depths of this particular sea
(ours, yours, we) —
not forgetting what its gifts are
slug, shore, sea and tide etc.

These single bones are difficult to space
if we had scrotums we would know their place
O drat these fish for nibbling
damn their eyes
damn their procreating
damn these thighs.

Some woman must have had a part in this
drat women
drat the jig-saw
drat the fish.

Try putting drat to scruples
damn these clues
all we find from man
is that he screws.

(aside) I have now recreated, silently,
        on the shores of
        Gitcheguma
        an exact replica of the framework
        of a man.
        It's milk-white now —
        and took some dredging for —
        took 30 years and each one was a bore
        and fruitless too
        by the look of him
        who's just a pile of bones
        (still life — with grin).
        If I had strength I'd huff upon his rib
        I'd have him up, about —
        but something's missing.

Back to the surface:
Where's the missing link?
Impound the flounder —
See That Boy Sink!

(aside) I check my links
        one link can spoil a chain
           with a hammer crack 'em and it's plain
        no weakness here
        I'd ride in any sea
        with chains like that
        and wouldn't worry either
        in the squall but one link's missing
        and that's flat.

As good as go
as good as gone —
some iron that!
(If man is what
he thinks he thinks —
I praise my Like
whose climate somehow stinks).

I couldn't dream a storm up
if I tried —
Wouldn't build an ocean
if I cried —
and as for pledging doubt
pledge truth as lies
pledge winning
as the final sad surprise.

Damn flotsam, jetsam,
damn this clinging wrack
I'd need a sieve to save
that bric-a-brac
and one sieve's holy
in a larger sea
(And One Hand's Trouble)
if it's digging past rot
you're after.

So —
kiss my omnipotence
and ask me no questions
(I'll tell you no lies)
like last to the bottom
is last to arise.

> *I'm not going near the water*
> *Am I being good?*
> *My body ain't flat iron*
> *And my soul ain't wood!*

(HIDDEN IN THE POEM ARE THE FIGURE, THE FO'C'S'LE,
THE LOSS OF A TOPS'L — SEE HOW MANY YOU CAN FIND.)

My Moll & Partner Joe

As my Moll & Partner Joe were stepping up to leave
the old black witch from somewhere else was tugging on my
sleeve
she was chanting spells above my ears and talking down her
hat
words about fidelity and the welcome on the mat
but my Moll & Partner Joe they were treading up the stair
there were flowers growing in his eyes and water in her hair.
The cardboard hard man troubled me — he was trying to insist
on holding up my fingers and bunching up my fist
by my Moll & Partner Joe they were dancing in the street
rainbows round their fingers and wings about their feet.
The iron fairy shuffled in — her halo round her eyes
she bore machineguns at her breasts and bombs between her
thighs
but my Moll & Partner Joe they were far too gone to miss
bolting up his parlour door they knew no more of this.
My gentle mistress welcomed me with garlands at her gate
I was bearing wreaths already and there was no time to wait
for my Moll & Partner Joe were by now being indiscreet
plucking ivy from the bedsprings — roses from the sheet.

The White Stallion

There was that horse
    that I found then
    my white one
big tall and lean as
    and mean as hell.

And people who saw me
    would stare as I passed them
and say
        'Look at him ...
    how he rides his cock-horse.'

But my steed
   the white stallion
stormed into the moonlight
   and on it was me.

There were those girls
   that I found then
   my loved ones
small fat and mean ones
   and virgins as well.

And those girls who saw me
   would weep as I passed them
   and cry
      'Look at him ...
   how he rides his cock-horse.'
But my steed
   the white stallion
went proud in the still night
   and on it was me.

There was one girl
   that I loved then —
   a woman —
as tall and as lithe as
   a woman should be.

And soon as I saw her
   I dismounted my stallion
   to stay
      by the woman
   whose love I required.
But my steed
   the white stallion
rode off in the moonlight
   and on it was she.

Goodbye to the horse
   to the woman
   and stallion.
Farewell to my cock-horse
   and loving as well.

To people who see me
   and stare as I pass them
   I wail
      'Look at me ...
   I once rode a cock-horse.'
But my steed
   the white stallion
is lost in the moonlight
   and on it rides she.

Why I Stroke the Cat

In 1939 my Father realised war was imminent —
strove to keep the family tree alive.
By 1940 I was one year old not five and twenty.
Father, bleeding in the dust of Alamein,
   sweating on the road toward Monte C,
      weeping in the mighty River Sangro.
I, the father's son, got the same feelings
   stuck below the belt —
longed for the day I had the girl I wanted.

Now, some twenty years later ...
                Father,
your picture is a decoration for my mantle-piece,
your body is a bundle of dry bones
yet I am closer to you than God.
Not that I was there when you charged the barricade —
I was too young to know.

But now I am beginning to understand that
we are both losers, Amigo, you and I.
So, let us lose together.
Lose at the public bar, downing whisky,
scheming the downfall of the green ginger-land virgin.
Having lost both there is nothing left to lose.
   Sir, you are my counsel and my camerado.

I have no argument
with the man who beats me at the chase.
I've had my furies, there's too much Mother in me —
good and noble — she has taught me how to lose too well.

The break that is forever
cannot be mended but by memory turning the hands.
Some guy way back told lies,
'The spirit lives it is the flesh that dies'.

O Padre mio,
I might yet make some money,
become tomorrow's Mr Neat and Square
and sprout a clean white collar every day,
become a father through the proper channels
but I shall never ever truly love.
I have my Mother's spirit and your gut —
spirit that helped to launch a thousand ships,
   that chained its body to steel rails,
     that reached out and touched the hem of
                   Winston Spencer Churchill.

That is why when I enter the citadel of love
    I cannot rant and rave,
    I cannot kiss her lips,
    I cannot stroke her golden hair.
It is not that I am a cat-fancier, do not think that,
it is just that having lost I have a loser's spirit
and it is easier if instead, I stooping,
stroke the cat.

My Enemies Have Sweet Voices

I was in a bar called Paradise
the fiddler from the band
                    asked me, 'Why do you stand
here crying?'
                    I answered him, 'Musician,
this may come as a surprise —
I was trying to split the difference
when it split before my eyes.'

> *My enemies have sweet voices*
> *their tones are soft and kind*
> *when I hear my heart rejoices*
> *and I do not seem to mind*

I was playing brag in Bedlam
the doctor wouldn't deal
                    asking, 'Why does he kneel
down weeping?'
                    I answered him, 'Physician,
I think you would have cried
I was falling back on failure
when the failure stepped aside.'

> *My enemies have sweet voices*
> *their tones are soft and kind*
> *when I hear my heart rejoices*
> *and I do not seem to mind*

I was blind side to the gutter
when Merlin happened by
                    asking, 'Why do you lie
there bleeding?'
                    I answered him, 'Magician,
as a matter of a fact
I was jumping to conclusions
when one of them jumped back.'

My enemies have sweet voices
their tones are soft and kind
when I hear my heart rejoices
and I do not seem to mind.

Wall

I built a cell of coolest stone
I did not build it exactly —
I made it what it was.

I stood inside it
a sun-coloured prisoner
in shackles of the purest gold
in milk-white chains
of ivory.

I fashioned for it
certain comforts —
hasps of saffron, walls of watchet,
a yoke of lapis lazuli.

I made the ceiling darkest blue:
Only the brighter stars shone through.

I built a cell of coolest stone:
Inside I stood like wood against the window
a band of white across my eyes.

God bless Peter, God bless Paul,
God bless everyone except the wall.

Part II

*Be not afeared
to encounter mountains
for thereby have many
encompassed molehills.*

List of the Pictures in Our House
(For Adrian Henri and P. P. Rubens)

I	A very beautiful escape executed by a fine artist in that style.	*100 florins*
II	Several goblins, painted from life, with nymphs in attendance.	*200 florins*
III	Bearded Lady with numerous Cherubs and one Troll.	*300 florins*
IV	'Stanley and His Curtain Raiser' — a stiff life retouched by my hand.	*400 florins*
V	The Vestal Virgins bearing garlands of bananas. Painted by my pupils.	*500 florins*
VI	Nude entitled 'Stanley's Last Encounter With The Sources of Evil'.	*600 florins*
VII	A self-portrait of Superboy. Entirely painted by my own hand.	NOT FOR SALE

Ring Song

Once upon a time there was a story
It was not a long story ...
It was a short story ...
A good story ...

It had neither a beginning, a middle
Or an end ...

First of all the story was told to a child —
The child smiled and said *'Tell me another'*

And the story was told to a man of influence —
The man of influence ignored it

The story was told to a critic —
The critic stuffed his shirt with it

The story was told to a theologian —
The theologian doubted

The story was told to a soldier —
The soldier tore off its wings
And wore them on his helmet

The story was told to a historian —
'These are not facts' said the historian

The story was told to a politician —
The politician also smiled but said nothing

The story was told to a government
Who debated it, amended it —
And, finally, refused to pass it

The story was told to a policeman —
The policeman took out his notebook

The story was told to a judge —
'What is a story?' asked the judge

The story was told to the hangman
Who wove it in his rope like hair

The story was told to a man in chains
Who made good his escape in it

The story was told to a juggler
Who threw it in the air and caught it
and threw it in the air and caught it
and threw it in the air ...

The story was told to an acrobat
Who suspended it below him

The story was told to a sculptor
Who hammered it into the shape of his mother

The story was told to a painter
Who signed it in the corner
And hung it on the wall

And the story was told to a man of the sea
Who opened the story and sailed out upon it

The story was told to a young girl
Whose mirror it became

The story was told to a bird —
The bird built a nest in its branches

And the story was told to a poet
And the poet passed on the story

And this was the story ...

Once upon a time there was a story
It was not a long story ...
It was a short story ...
A good story ...

It had neither a beginning, a middle
Or an end ...

Obituary

On July first aged eighty-six
Mr John Theophilus Rix
After some months sickness.
Mr Rix is remembered well
For his jewellers shop in Clerkenwell.
A craftsman in the dying art
Of picking time apart.
Apprenticed first to Golstein Lee
He bought them out in '23
And moved to John Street, EC1.
His present business carries on
Without him.

Mr Rix, Mr Rix, the nation's last watchmaker
Made his name with a pocketful of ticks
For the Governor of Jamaica.

Mr Rix, Mr Rix, so his family say
By contemplating dandelions
Could tell the time all day.

Although he made his last watch in 1944
We hear that he had just begun
Attempts to make one more.

A craftsman at a dying art
He picked his time apart.

'Yes', I said, 'but is it Art?'

Took me to the battlefield
saw the mushroom cloud
said 'We can see the colours even
when our heads are bowed'.
Showed me the destruction
the slaughter à la carte
said 'Isn't Nature wonderful'.
'Yes', I said
'but is it Art?'

Took me to the scientist
opened up a phial
said 'This is only chicken-pox
and rhino bile.'
Showed me what it did to mice
said 'That's just a start
but isn't Nature wonderful.'
'Yes,' I said
'but is it Art?'

Took me to the hospital
pulled aside the sheet
said 'Look at that pulsating
listen to the beat.'
Showed me the incision
threw away the heart
said 'Isn't Nature wonderful.'
'Yes,' I said
'but is it Art?'

Took me to the tenement
opened every door
said 'Have you seen the copulation
practised by the poor?
We select the ones to breed
and we reject a part
but isn't Nature wonderful.'

'Yes,' I said
'but is it Art?'

Took me to the prison
threw away the key
said 'If you learn our lesson
you could still be free.'
Pointed out the spy holes
and my adaptation chart
said 'Isn't Nature wonderful?'

'Yes,' I said.

Bang, Mister
(A Poem For Peace, Believe Me)

I fight slow wars
like Vietnam
all day —
see 12th Cav G.I.s
in the Palais de Danse
on cold November nights.
I fight slow wars
up the Great North Road —
see Viet Cong
in the cabs of innumerable
long-distance lorries
that don't stop.

I was born in war
I was a war baby
nurtured on war
I had a six-shot rattle
a silver Smith & Wesson spoon
a scarlet skittle that spelt death
and a tongue that shot *bang bang*
at appropriate nurses.

When I fell I was brave
like Monty
and smiled all the way
to the ambulance.

I had a happy childhood
I came in on a wing and a prayer
and — *phew!* — made it.
I heard Vera Lynn
singing, 'We'll Meet Again'
and believed her.
I read Hotspur
and was Orde Wingate
patrolling for Japs
in the British jungle
where my death lurked
behind every dandelion.

I had a Johnny Victory Super Gun
an Action Man packed with
inactivity.
A steel helmet made from
real plastic
and a tongue that sang *bang bang*
when it meant to say
Ich liebe dich.

I hung out the washing
    on the Siegfried Line —
found none of the dirty
    linen was mine.

I kept the home fires burning
and watched the slow flames
devour my parents.
I kept a constant lookout
for bluebirds over white cliffs

and saw the warm birds fall
into the wild sea.
I slept in my own little room again
and suffered terrible insomnia —
constant nightmares of Peace.

I saw Peace
I saw the Mothers rejoicing
I watched the Fathers returning
I watched the singing and dancing
I watched the dervishes in the streets
of soft melting flowers
and I sang *bang bang*.

On the outbreak of hostilities
I enlisted in the Enemies of Peace
and became a prisoner of POW!
I have seen the bright boys burn
I have seen the maidens weep
I have examined the silver
in my teeth and lied
God is on my side.

I have equated mushroom soup with The Bomb
I have eaten hand-grenades at hot-dog stalls
I have held up countless maidens with a 303 banana
I have watched the children eat their candy phosph.
and seen Biggles fall from a clear sky
to spill their warm blood
upon the cobble stones
of death.

I have danced the dance of death
with flagsellers
on flag day.
I have danced the hell-trot
through the foxholes
of Flanders.

I have danced the Tango
with sweet war maidens
to the bren's staccato
till the blood ran
into their
hearts.

I have been handed flowers
and seen the walls bloom guns.
I have been exhorted to make love
and I have made it too.
Yes, I have made love —
with a soft bayonet
on searchlit beaches.
I have been told that Love is Peace
but I have made love
I know about love
love is not peace.

I have smelt the stench of death
and found it sweet.
I have smelt the scent of orange blossom
and preferred mustard.
I have considered the world's explosive ultimate
and turned with a whimper into the still night
shouting — *Bang, Mister.*

I have prayed for the next great war
to carve me off into its death and gory
shouting — *Bang, Mister.*

Sillysuit

This is a sillysuit I wear
an elbow through
the seat threadbare
and I don't know where
I'll wear it again.

I wore it to the Palace
when they told me that the Queen
was hiding in the ivy
somewhere inbetween
the East Wing and the West Wing.

I wore it to the Castle
when they handed out the arms
and I heard the choristers
singing the psalms —
up to their thighs in ammunition.

I wore it to the Chapel
where the men were on their knees
praying to whatever gods
and all saying please —
as blue as their eyes the salvation.

I wore it to the brewery
I wore it to the fair
I wore it to make love in
And I wore it everywhere.

So Stitch & Snippit tailorman
cut another suit
sew it in the latest style
and let the trumpets toot
there is one reveille
I won't answer.

This is a billet-doux I bear
signed by Her Majesty
and that's quite rare
but I don't have a care
to wear that
again.

They Don't Make Dynamite in Big Sticks
(A Hymn For The New Scottish Religion)

You fling enough Love
and some of it sticks
Can't crack planets with stones
You can't fight wars with fiddlesticks
Spent a long time trying —
Failed.

Daisy chains, Daisy chains,
You can't bind dragons in dreams.

You need good straw
to make good bricks
Can't screw kisses from bones
You can't mix peace with politics
Spent a long time trying —
Failed.

Daisy chains, Daisy chains,
You can't bind dragons in dreams.

Elegy for Arthur Prance —
'The Man Who Taught The Stars To Dance'

The toes that tapped through morning air
were once stand-ins for Fred Astaire.
The heels cool in the gutter where
the dancer lies up-ended.

The one time only Arthur Prance —
'The Man Who Taught The Stars To Dance' —
had reached his zenith with a jig
which once came over very big
on radio.

The feet that clicked from ten flights high
and danced flamenco down the sky
had once made Ginger Rogers cry
'His *entrechat* is splendid.'

    The one time only Arthur Prance —
    'The Man Who Taught The Stars To Dance' —
    possessed an act of wide appeal
    especially his eightsome reel
    danced alone.

    The one time only Arthur Prance —
    'The Man Who Taught The Stars To Dance' —
    performed his final pirouette
    and heard applause he didn't get.

Music: 'Lover's Leap'
Sister O'Broin Jump Band
HMV AS2175 (Issued 1936)

'I Hate the Shape of the Human Head'
(For Alan Jackson, who said it)

iron knives
iron knives
show the shape of human lives

        don't give me no
        iron knives
        don't give me no
        human lives

guns of metal
guns of steel
show the flaw in the human heel

> *don't give me no*
> *guns of steel*
> *don't give me no*
> *human heel*

domes of wire
domes of lead
show the shape of the human head

> *don't give me no*
> *domes of lead*
> *that show the shape*
> *of the human head*

My Lords, Ladies, and Gentlemen —

The Meat Work Saga!

In the Red Corner
weighing in at 168 lbs —
MEAT!

In the Blue Corner
weighing in at 168 lbs —
MEAT!

1

SECONDS OUT
ROUND ONE

(BELL)

168 lbs of meat
can look good —
168 lbs of meat
can smile —
168 lbs of meat
can dance —
168 lbs of meat
throws a shadow —
168 lbs of meat
can be red, white,
black, brown or yellow —
168 lbs of meat
is a target —
168 lbs of meat
can get serious —
168 lbs of meat
can throw its weight
about —
168 lbs of meat
can turn nasty —
168 lbs of meat
can kill!

(BELL)

2

SECONDS OUT
ROUND TWO

(BELL)

168 lbs of meat
acknowledges its own
existence —
168 lbs of meat
can make love —
168 lbs of meat
can bleed —
168 lbs of meat
can do it for the money —
168 lbs of meat
is 70% water —
168 lbs of meat
incredibly, works —
168 lbs of meat
can be stoned
      is stoned
      and will be stoned —
168 lbs of meat
loves money, blood,
other meat and stones —
168 lbs of meat
can squeak —
168 lbs of meat
is chicken!

3

SECONDS OUT
ROUND THREE

(BELL)

168 lbs of meat
can be kosher —
168 lbs of meat
can get crucified —
168 lbs of meat
can also trip —
168 lbs of meat
believes in flags
.   frontiers,
.   and meat —
168 lbs of meat
can save money,
.   stamps,
.   mementoes,
anything —
but not itself —
168 lbs of meat
can be worth its weight
in steel shares —
168 lbs of meat
can be worth
less —
168 lbs of meat
can be torn by doubt —
168 lbs of meat
can sink or swim —
168 lbs of meat
can die *oblique stroke* will die!

(BELL)

4

SECONDS OUT
ROUND FOUR

(BELL)

168 lbs of meat
can get up and win —
168 lbs of meat
can give in —
168 lbs of meat
can be a born loser —
168 lbs of meat
can turn' the tables —
168 lbs of meat
can win friends and influence meat —
The best friend of 168 lbs of meat
is 14 lbs of meat *(sic)* —
The worst enemy of 168 lbs of meat
is 168 lbs of meat *(Q.E.D.)* —
168 lbs of meat
has seven holes *(E. & O.E.)* —
168 lbs of meat
can be the light
but when it is
it isn't —
168 lbs of meat
can dream —
càn't it?

(BELL)

5
SECONDS OUT
ROUND FIVE

(BELL)

Part III

*Glass eyes
are worse than useless
to musicians.
Again, there is a place —
even for white violins —
in the houses of
the blind.*

We

we are not a ferris wheel
we don't spin

we left them dancing
as best they could
still living in the egg
still fighting
the shell

and soon the small stars
were captured in the heels
of children

everywhere the pods smiled
like wounds
and the seeds fell
like stones
in the immaculate air

and the mothers wondered
at the taste of dust

and the children stopped the dance
the stars unrecognisable

we went into the forest
to hunt wood

we never hear the wheel revolve
we hear it
when it
stops

In Which I Sing His Life and Times

Though one of his gifts
was the gift of a rose
they have accepted nothing.

Although it heralded undoubted beauty
they looked past its bloom, its fragrance
and saw only its thorn.

Again he returned
bearing gifts of thistles.

This is how they approached him —
smiling, acceptable,
holding out their fingers.

That is where they went to —
their fingers in their mouths,
their smiles fading at their body's puzzlement.

It is from that safe distance that they sing
their little songs of roses, roses.

The Rainbow Knight's Confession

My armour *becomes* me.
I have it to the letter now —
even the colour of my steed,
a much deliberated
white.

> When black becomes the colour of the good
> I shall ride black.
> In the meantime
> piebalds are for taking.

My helmet is of *catholic* proportions —
nothing fancy — just the stoutest tin
and not too loud for roustabouts to clang.

My visor's of an intricate design —
so I see out and no one else sees in.

    I carry colours more than arms
    but that is for the better
    if there's challenge in the air.
    My colours won't offend —
    with rainbows there.

    I change my colour for my company —
    a purple knight sees purple in my cloth
    a yellow knight sees yellow
    blue knight blue
    the blackest knights I raise my visor to.

I wear my stirrups midway
from my girth — wanting not
to offend the gentlemen of court
who tell the talents of a man
from being short on strappage
else too long, and therefore foolish —
and all of that through armour.

There is no doubt I cut a pretty rig
I am saluted more than I salute —
which is as it should be.

My breast-plate is most carefully prepared
with daily rubs of talcum and such tricks.
I make not too much noise —
with oils from Persia I have learnt
to cut out all my jangle, squeak and clank.
I hear more times than I am heard.

I have my hauberk metalled to a T
and all in all the time is going well.
Only in my private chambers
do I stand apart from this.
I place my armour in the corner then
or else I'm working on its gleam.

O sure, this armour's only implement
I mind my body too —
rub oils in that
and pare it where it grows.
I bathe it daily,
daily shave my chin.

There's nothing else except the hair of it
and I have learnt a trick or two with that —
I comb it, where it grows, across my horns.

And The Next Object Is

1
To the left of Calico Rose
a new hole dominates the horizon.
A new hole of infinitesimal proportions
dominates, like a tower —

> *not the GPO Hole*
> *not the Eiffel Hole*
> *not the Empire State Hole*
> *not the Leaning Hole of Pisa —*

This ...
            the Glory Hole of Calico Rose —
a new hole
a pin-prick
that requires no foundations.

This Morning Glory whole
a monument — with no external shadows —
to Calico Rose

a hole is a hole is a hole is a hole
a Calico Rose is a Calico Rose

A new hole —
and therefore worthy of your worship —
for here's a hole where never was a whole

    A hole that is as good as new
    a hole that's as clean as an amputation
    a hole that encourages a cat's ninth life
    a hole that is as distant as your eyelashes
        and as close as the next rain ...
    a hole to encourage the swelling of wombs
    a hole to scrub pomegranates by —
    a hole to undermine sepulchres
    a hole to teach children to count up to one on ...

    O holy holy holy
    loud sing the end of
    tedium

for the hole — the new whole —
has finally been dug
the monument's complete ...

    Laudeamus Sing Delirium

    Beware landslides
    Beware the heavy rain
    Beware the march of human feet
    Beware the diviner of new waters
    Beware the single elephant (and herds)
    Beware the roadmakers, the bridge builders
        the coughers of industry —

Don't believe everything you read in 'Tit-Bits' —
for the kingdom of the hole is at hand
now is the season of our crimson suns
the summer of our discontent —

the skies are full of acrobats.

2
The lion-tamer puts his head
in the lion's mouth

Me —
    I just place two fingers
into Mother Earth —

        Chacun à son Cirque.
        Chacun à son Monument.

        Calico Rose arose
        from José —

a blue cornflower emerges from her monument.
Within the confines of Fort Knox — a small earthquake.
The disgusting aroma of unused money pervades the precincts
the petals of the flower are the colour of bank-notes
the backs of all its leaves are green

        beside it —
        a new hole of infinitesimal proportions
        dominates —
        like a cornflower!

Upside down across the sky
an ice-blue aeroplane scrawls the message
    TARZAN'S TRIPES FOR EVER
A white parachute flutters from the aeroplane:

Calico Rose arose
as an international star of the non-ferrous metal market ...

    She is dropping leaflets bearing the names of Presidents
    She is signing her name on irresponsible documents
    She is singing ALL YOU LOVE IS NEED
    She is keeping spirits bright —

    She believes in fairies and policemen.

3

Canaries visit the depths of holes in order to determine
the absence or the presence of after damp. At the rim of the
monument a child is preaching gentle revolution — 'Each single
pubic hair,' he says, 'is worth its weight in Gold.'

    So Socrates has pocketed the rock —
    undiscovered flowers break from his fingers
    tender virgins find hemlock growing
        in their opening mouths
    the leaders of nations tear old photographs
        from family albums
        and hold them before their faces
    Joan of Arc burns with a new fire
    and in Paris two millionaires meet (in an old definition)
        their pockets inside out.

The Israelites march gladly through the streets of Jerusalem
        unfolding themselves like roses
the whole cry of Harlem is *'Wham Bam, Thank you Ma'am'*
and finally the dancers inherit the party political system
        the lotus eaters re-appear as prophets ...

    Prophets with moonrock embellishing their navels
Prophets with purple mandalas engraved on their foreheads
    Prophets who are used to decorate processions
        in honour of new holes

Prophets who are used as statues, which —
    for the first time —
    celebrate more than robes
And ...
    in accordance with their teaching
we listen for the songs of yellow birds and hear only
Rachel's mourning — that, and the indelicate footsteps
    of Lot's Wife.

4
But now we hear ...

We hear the index finger of every right hand/in every corner of
the land/creak and straighten/and we hear the mighty move-
ment of Mother Earth as every finger

    (ALTOGETHER NOW)

    prods a new hole into
Mother Earth/and we feel the warmth creeping up our arms/to
our elbows/to our arm-pits/to our shoulders/to our hip bones/
until it pervades our whole bodies/and each hole is a monument
to our bodies/and each hole contains its own peculiarities/the
roots of trees/the droppings of animals/earth/leaf-mould/frag-
ments of our forefathers/dust/diamonds/the beginnings of
mines/sometimes, even, bits of ourselves ...

    and some will undoubtedly mine their holes
some will dig deeper   some will explore their holes
    some may inhabit their holes
    some will say 'There's nothing in it'

    but some will say:
'I maketh a new hole which I shall praise for it is new
    and there's a whole where never was a hole
    and something good *could* come of this.'

    And the next object is, A Calico Rose ...
    A Calico Rose.

I Think of This As Something for the Sun

Take this tree
on which is carved a heart and several arrows
Take this pin
on the head of which is inscribed the Lord's Prayer
Take this knife
on which are written the names of the twelve apostles
Take this pomegranate.

Take the tree
and sit beneath it
Take the knife
and cut the pomegranate
Take the pin
and seed by seed, eat the fruit.

Then — when you have picked the husk quite clean —
you put away the tree
the knife, the pin
and think of this as something for the sun.

From That It Rose
(For Martin)

See, I have built for you
a wall.
I did not *want* a wall,
did not *conceive* it.
Simply,
I had demolished the wall
that I was given and found —
behind me —
the beginnings of a wall.
On that I built.
From that it rose.

With this gift you may achieve something
or nothing.
You may hate the wall,
You may come to love the wall,
You may scale it.
From its eaves you will get a better
or a worse view. That,
you will not know
till you have scaled it.

You may stand off and admire the wall,
You may examine its dark interiors,
You may peer through its chinks to the far side
or — alternatively —
You may walk round to the far side
and peer through its chinks to
the far side.
Either way,
You will not see yourself more clearly.

You will take refuge in it,
You will beat your head against it,
already you have felt its heavy hand.

You may hide it from your friends and enemies
or you may show it to your friends and enemies
in the hope that they might understand.
Ask them to show you their walls
so that you might understand.

    I have built for you a wall —
    not perfect but a wall.
    It teeters strangely.
    In rain it will appear to cry,
    at times it will appear to hear —
    its fissures open.
    You may examine its construction
    and find it wanting —
    be grateful, it will be easier to demolish.

I have built for you a wall.
In it there are many stones —
some are new — you will know them easily.
In your fingers they will turn to pain.

> *Do not let these stones be taken*
> *for they may be used against you.*
> *Keep them, use them against others.*
> *Use them against me.*

Some stones are old stones —
these I have salvaged from my father's wall.
They are good stones —
hard as flint and cumbersome.
I took them, used them.
Take them, use them.

> *Do not use them for effect as I did.*
> *Use them where they are most use.*
> *Bury them beneath the earth.*

You will find old stones that shine like diamonds.
Use them where they will show
or where they will not show.

It will be better if you plan your wall.
Include the better stones from mine.
Include, if possible,
the key stone in the key position.
That way — when time for demolition comes —
your wall will fall more readily.

Beware my wall.
Watch it carefully.
Take care it does not hit you.
Do not trust it with your weight.
Do not trust it with the weight of others.
Do not trust it.
When time for demolition comes
work downwards from the top.

Take care. Take care.
Already I have heard your hands' light work
clinking at my cold foundations.

Monsieur Sévère in a Black Hat

M. Sévère in a black hat
is holding little Pierre
by the lobe of his left ear.

Little Pierre is standing on tippy-toes
to relieve the pain which M. Sévère
is undoubtedly causing.

But, M. Sévère is — at heart —
a good man. He is teaching
little Pierre his French
verbs.

Poor M. Sévère is unaware
that our friend is in some
pain.

M. Sévère is unaware of little Pierre.
Little Pierre is unaware of M. Sévère.

It will take more than tippy-toes
to relieve the pain that one
is undoubtedly causing
to the other.

Enter Quince with Script of Play

In the clearing the naked dwarf
has made his umpteenth
entrance.

Entrances are his strong
point. He is a poor leaver —
makes unnoticeable
exits.

Immediately the acrobat stops
his *mon-ot-on-ous*
knees-bend
and peers down his nose
at the source of interruption.

The circle of demons sit
among the ragwort and columbine
until, at a nod from the acrobat,
they leap upon the dwarf,
kill him, and throw his harsh body
in the undergrowth.

That was a good exit, Shortie.

Now we await your next entrance.

From **I See You on My Arm**
(for Kate)

1 Abandoned Poem

I build you a tower —
  it shall be overthrown.
I share your mirror —
  it shall break into seven slivers.
I give you a valley —
  it shall be overcome by many waters.
I show you a loud sun, the sky booms black.

This poem is a boat, my Love.

I know. I know. I know.

'ABANDON POEM'

*Abandon Poem
and go.*

2 Paper, Stone, Steel

Behind my back
I make Paper —

You make Steel.

Steel cuts Paper.

Behind my back
I make Stone —

You make Paper.

Paper wraps Stone.

Behind my back
I make Steel —

You make Stone.

Stone blunts Steel.

Paper and Paper are equal
Stone and Stone are equal
Steel and Steel are equal

Steel cuts Paper
Paper wraps Stone
Stone blunts Steel

Behind my back
I make rain —

Behind your back
You cup your hands.

3 Abracadabra

I
From my sleeve
I conjure up
Five loaves
And two fishes.

That's it.
That's what we want.

Now do you say you love me?

II

From my sleeve
I conjure up
A new moon
In a new heaven.

That's it.
That's what we want.

Now will you leave us alone?

4 I Be The Root

Between the *Thoughts of Chairman Mao*
and the postcard of Glen Sligachan
stands the little orange tree
that we have moved two hundred miles
from Scotland to England.

Even here it is not at home —
it gives no shade,
it bears no fruit,
no bird nests in its branches.

When there is Sun
we give it Sun.
When there is Moon
its oiled leaf glimmers
in our darkness.

I be the root,
I be the leaf,
I be the green stalk —
You be the bell jar.

5 I See You on My Arm

I see you on my arm:

My arm of contention
My arm of indelicate action
My arm of disillusion

I see you on my arm:
My marrowed arm —

My arm of swastikas
My arm of evil, evil, evil
My arm of the predictable colour —
Black

I see you on my arm:
My weather arm —

My arm of hope
My arm of doubt
My arm of disarray
My arm of both the opening
And closing

I see you on my arm:

My arm of dust
My arm of death

My arm of earth, to earth.

I see you on my sleeve.

And The Grey Mare Being The Better Steed

It was quick and easy
an easy choice to take
best to ride the better steed
and the grey mare being the better steed
an easy choice to make.

It was nice and easy
an easy chance to break
best to take the softer fall
and the short fall being the softer fall
an easy fall to fake.

It was free and easy
an easy life to take
best to kill the fatter calf
and the fat calf being the fatter calf
an easy feast to make.